Eros, Love & Sexuality

Also by John C. Pierrakos, M.D.
CORE ENERGETICS
Developing the Capacity to Love and Heal

JOHN C. PIERRAKOS, M.D.

EROS, LOVE & SEXUALITY
The Forces That Unify
Man & Woman

LIFERHYTHM

Produced in the LifeRhythm Energy Field
Editor: Peter Greenwood
Type Layout & Design: Teja Gerken
Cover Design: Siegmar Gerken with Fred Hageneder
at Dragon Design
Coordinator: Dixie Black Shipp

Cover photograph of The Kiss *by Rodin used*
by special arrangement with the Tate Gallery, London

Library of Congress Cataloging-in-Publication Data
Pierrakos, John C.
  Eros, love & sexuality : the forces that unify man & woman / by
  John C. Pierrakos.
  128 p.   cm.
  ISBN 0-949795-05-1 (hardcover).
  1. Man-woman relationships. 2. Love. 3. Sex (Psychology).
  4. Mind and body. 5. Bioenergetics. I. Title
  HQ801.P575 1997   97-28378
  306.7--dc21   CIP

Printed in the United States of America

For the light she brought to my life, and in memory of the powerful love that connected our hearts, I dedicate this book to Eva, my soul mate, my co-worker, and my dearest friend. The flow of our eros, love and sexuality transformed my life.

ACKNOWLEDGMENTS

I express my deep appreciation to editor Peter Greenwood for his dedicated help in developing and writing the text for this book. His clear vision brought clarity and focus to the material; his interest, care, and love were an invaluable encouragement.

I am grateful to those colleagues of mine who so generously gave their time to help me integrate my thoughts, which in turn developed and matured the content of this book.

And to my colleague, Siegmar Gerken Ph.D., I express gratitude for his helpful comments on the material, his loving guidance throughout the process, and his commitment to the work.

CONTENTS

PREFACE

The dynamic forces of *energy* and *consciousness* are the essence of life. They are manifested in everything that exists whether it be in the furthest reaches of the cosmos or in the depths of the human soul. These forces shape the body and create the personality; they are the forces of our evolutionary process and the deepest expression of God within us.

Energy permeates and shapes all existence. It is an indivisible unity that manifests as a powerful movement in every aspect of our life. It knows the truth, it lives in the now. The force of consciousness is our connection with our soul and it is expressed through the mind, that which knows, wills, and acts.

In the human realm, energy and consciousness manifest themselves as eros, love, and sexuality. Like the atmospheric jetstreams that swirl around the earth, these three forces are always present. They surround us; our consciousness connects with them as it expands and reaches toward the essence of their movement. Thus eros, love, and sexuality bring movement, vibration, and expansion to us; they provide the possibility of unifying our dualistic state. By allowing these forces to enter our daily existence we bring creativity and joy to our lives.

Eros is the *transformative* force of life, love is the *unifying* force and sexuality is the *creative* force—the expression of our physical nature. They need a constant commitment to truth in our quest for fulfillment. This book explores these forces and how we block them in our personality and in our body. Confronting these obstacles is our greatest challenge. It is our life task, an especially difficult one since love does not arise spontaneously within us but is rather the expression of a conscious will to evolve toward a unified being. To bring out our love we must commit to an honest exploration

of both the positive and negative aspects of our personality.

To love another we must love ourselves; we must
heal the split within. Eros, sexuality, and love—especially love—present the possibility of unifying the masculine and feminine within each one of us and at the
same time allow us to unify our soul with another being. This is the path toward unification of our dualistic
state.

In this brief book, I have tried to present an enor-
mously complex process in a simple and direct way. My
hope is that it will encourage you to allow love to guide
you on your voyage through life.

THE PRINCIPLES OF
CORE ENERGETICS

L ife is movement—we breathe, we eat, we walk—
we move! Emotions flow through our body,
thoughts flow through our mind; the flow of daily life,
moving freely, is an experience that creates pleasure.
There is however, another aspect essential to human life:
an awareness of this movement, a *conscious* experience
of it. The combination of these two, *energy* (movement)
and *consciousness* creates the possibility of pleasure, joy,
and ecstasy.

We are born to experience pleasure, love and joy
in every form—in our sexuality, our creativity, and in
our union with the universal spirit. Although the expe-

rience of pleasure is our true natural function, many people choose pain. Why? When we're in pain we still have control of the ego; it's safer than pleasure which is a threat to our ego control.

EROS, LOVE & SEXUALITY

The unobstructed flow of the three great forces of life—eros, love, and sexuality—creates the most important source of pleasure. These three forces are simply different aspects of the life force, but when they flow freely they are experienced as one. They generate all activity, all creativity. We feel this force when we are moved by a symphony, a beautiful sunset, or love for another.

Eros is the awakening force that transforms our defenses, our negative beliefs and the distorted feelings that imprison us. Almost everyone, at least once in his or her life, has been led by eros to an experience of unification. Whenever we are excited, whether by a vista of snow-capped mountains or by another human being, it is eros that creates the excitement. This force appears as a *vibrational resonance.* In other words, two energy systems, one of which must be human, vibrate sympathetically.

If this vibrational resonance occurs between two human beings a connection is made and their energies expand and begin to fuse. They feel a warmth throughout their bodies and in their hearts. As their life energy connects they experience vibration, movement; they surpasss the boundaries of ordinary reality. A new perception puts them in touch with the divine. This is the force of eros at work.

Love is the omnipresent force of the universe; it *unifies* energy and consciousness. Unlike the forces of eros and sexuality which have both active and inactive states, love remains the constant, unvarying force of life. Whereas eros is a gift from without, we must work for love: it is an energy and a feeling that follows our will. Love arises from a deep caring and an honest exploration of our own and of another person's feelings, the mystery and splendor of his or her being. To love, we must believe that our partner, despite distortions, has unique qualities that will lead to spiritual union. Genuine love is an expression of happiness.

Sexuality is the great force of creation. The free movement of this force produces pleasure. Sexuality, however, is not limited to the physical relationship between two partners; it permeates every activity of our life. Blockage of the sexual force deeply affects relationships, fulfillment in work, creativity, and the development of our spiritual self.

ENERGY AND CONSCIOUSNESS

The three aspects of the life force—sexuality, eros, and love—have two dimensions: *energy* and *consciousness.* They are the foundation of our existence. Energy and consciousness are in a continual state of interaction: energy is shaped and directed by consciousness which is itself driven by energy.

Energy and consciousness operate at all levels of personal reality: *body, mind, feelings,* and *spirit.* Scientists and philosophers tend to limit consciousness to the mind and energy to the body. This belief narrows understanding and restricts creativity. Western religions attend to the spirit, but ignore the body and misperceive feeling while Eastern disciplines, yoga, for example, focus on the body and spirituality but deny feelings. These splits not only fragment our personal lives but our perception of reality as well.

Core Energetics seeks to restore all the dimensions of personal reality to a *unified* state. In effect, we seek a unified theory of humanity, much as physics seeks a unified field theory on the nature of material reality. This perspective has the potential to reunify philosophy, science, religion, education and the healing arts.

Energy is the very stuff of which we are made. At a microscopic level, scientists have found it impossible to distinguish between energy and matter. Depending on one's perspective, things seem to be waves of energy or particles of matter. Our body, our entire being is composed of radiant energy, an energy so powerful that it casts a visible aura (energy field) around the physical body. This energy cannot be destroyed, but it can be accelerated, decelerated, altered, or distorted.

Consciousness shapes and directs the energy that flows within us. Consciousness is virtually limitless, but we impose limitations on it by relegating it to the mind alone. The body has its own consciousness, its own wisdom. We do not have to will it to breathe, to pump blood, to digest food, or to defend against disease. Nor, if we are free of illusion, must we consciously decide what to do when a real threat occurs. The wisdom of the body takes over; we respond instinctively with a natural self-regulated rhythm.

Feelings also have consciousness. In a joyful moment our mind doesn't stop to say, "Now I'm happy." If we are feeling loss, the mind doesn't say, "I'm sad, now it's time to cry." These feelings arise and flow spontaneously because they are deeply conscious of the nature of our inner reality.

But our spiritual self posesses the greatest consciousness of all. It has the power to choose the right answer from a myriad of possibilities, to guide us along the road, to avoid evil, to seek what is good. Our spiritual self is expressed in all the manifestations of love. Spirituality is the expansion of consciousness without limits.

THE EGO MASK

Our perception of the lower self and the core is blocked by the critical ego. This ego is a defense of our unconscious negativities. It enables us to suppress, then forget, the negative emotions of our childhood. Many of us have experienced scenes like this:

> Mother walks into her child's room and, finding the eight-year-old on the bed masturbating, says, "Stop that right now! It's disgusting—don't do that." The child tries to stifle the desire for this pleasure but its energy will not be denied. The child attempts to preserve this sensual gratification eventually lead to various forms of "misbehavior." When scolded, he or she screams back, *"I hate you!"* Mother replies, "Good children do not yell at their mother!"

Now the child has learned that pleasure is "bad" therefore any release of energy *must* be bad. It resorts to deception. The child begins to create a defense—a mask—an idealized self-image that affirms self-worth and placates the intrusive parent. This mask, a thin, brittle layer, hides the powerful energy of the negative unconscious. Perhaps the mask is one of aloofness. Or hostility, rebellion, competence, helplessness. Out of this survival strategy is born a personality.

THE LOWER SELF—CONSCIOUS AND UNCONSCIOUS NEGATIVE STATES

Deep within us we carry a negative state of emotions which we bring to this life along with our positive emotions, physical traits and other characteristics. These emotions are usually violent and destructive, permeated by rage, hate, and cruelty. We are generally not conscious of our *lower self;* it remains hidden when we appear to be well adjusted. It absorbs great quantities of our energy and is expressed indirectly through our mask personality and directly in times of crisis when we feel threatened and not in control. Because we're ashamed of the lower self, we find it very diffcult to reveal it and to express its negative feelings without judging and blaming ourselves. We feel that this exposure will wipe out our positive attributes and leave only the negativity of the lower self.

The lower self must be transformed in order for us to develop. When we become conscious of the lower self and accept this part of ourselves, when we find the courage to say, "I'm cruel, I want to hurt you, I want to punish you," a great part of the transformational process has begun.

We keep a great deal of our energy stored in the lower self because we fear pleasure and our positive feelings. We feel that if we're positive, we'll be vulnerable. The lower self is one aspect of our duality: the other is our creative core. Therefore we need to explore the lower self to free ourselves from its bondage—to transform its energy into the creative self, the *core*.

THE CORE

Each one of us has a center, a core of divine wisdom and energy. Here, energy and consciousness are wholly pure, luminous, and unfettered. Energy radiates from this core as it does from the heart of a star, moving through our entire being, enlivening every molecule. The task of Core Energetics is to help the individual contact the boundless resources of the core and release them in order to create a life of pleasure, dignity, and freedom.

Through the core, we are connected to all things, all the energy of the cosmos. The core is the source of our being; it is our divine connection with the universal forces. We know it by many names: Christ consciousness, Buddha nature, God. The core embraces love, wisdom, compassion, and pleasure. When we allow ourselves to be moved by our core energies, we need rely on nothing else. Everything we need for pleasure and fulfillment resides here in the center of our being as close to us and as readily available as our hands, our ears, our eyes. As we activate the qualities of our core we bring out the higher self.

The following illustration of the core and the layers that surround and occlude it is not a literal representation of our consciousness and personality. It is an attempt to depict energy forms, not matter as we normally perceive it; the core and the other layers depicted here are aspects of every particle of our being:

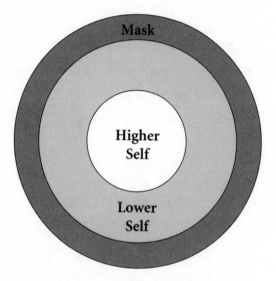

Dimensions of Consciousness

The core is the center of love. All the manifestations of love can be seen as a connection with our spirituality. When we allow it, the rhythm and boundless energy of the core permeate our entire being. Here, in our radiant core, there is complete unification of the duality of life; here reside omniscience, continuity and wisdom. Our work in Core Energetics is to transform and overcome the obstacles that prevent us from experiencing our core.

THE FIVE LEVELS OF PERSONALITY

Together, energy and consciousness create our personality. Core Energetics divides the personality into five levels, or components, as represented by this pyramid:

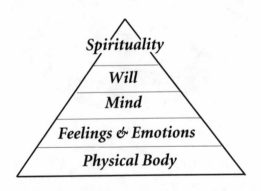

Dimensions of Personality

THE BODY

Supporting the entire structure is the physical body, the vessel of our soul, the laboratory of our life. The body is permeated by pulsatory waves of life energy: as a sculptor molds the clay, so does our consciousness use this life energy to shape the body. The active, shaping aspect represents the male principle while the mold itself represents the female principle.

Most of us carry chronic tension in various parts of our body which block creativity and pleasure. If we're born with a healthy body we have a great fountain of energy—we react spontaneously to life. But this spontaneity is often stifled by our parents and a culture that inhibits free expression. When you say *no* to the life force, you say no to life. You inevitably create a block somewhere in your body: knees, pelvis, stomach, chest, throat, etc. These blocks appear as aches and pains in the legs, back, and neck, etc. because the river of energy flows ceaselessly within the body and it cannot be stopped without suffering severe consequences.

This physical pain means you are not acknowledging the truth about yourself, your hatred, your cruelty—

your **NO!** Furthermore, you do not keep this pain to yourself, you also give it to those around you.

EMOTIONS/FEELINGS

An emotion—hate, anger, jealousy, affection and so on—is a general state, a concept. A feeling is a current that flows through us and causes us to *feel* angry or loving in a particular way about someone or something that affects our life. A feeling is uniquely of the moment; it has no name but we can usually categorize it as one emotion or another— love, hate, anger, etc.

Personal development requires that we work with both our positive and negative emotions; they are the truth of the soul. When we take responsiblity for our hate, our cruelty, we have acknowledged the truth and begun the journey of self-transformation. Because we were not allowed free expression of these feelings as children we think it's wrong to have negative feelings. When they arise, we feel unworthy. The first step out of this dilemma is to recognize these feelings without blaming yourself, to physically feel the rhythm of all your feelings, feel the sadness as it washes through you, feel the joy as it leaps and dances.

MIND/THOUGHT

The world of the mind creates art, science, philosophy and many other marvels of our civilization. Our thoughts, however, are dominated by distorted images from our early years. A corporate executive who controls international business empires passes a short, dark woman on the street and is suddenly overwhelmed by a feeling of powerlessness—she reminds him of his mother. This is an example of the kind of persistent image that forms our belief systems. If a woman believes she doesn't deserve love, she will be unable to develop a relationship based on love; if a man believes he doesn't deserve to be happy he will create conditions in his life that keep happiness away.

WILL

Our will is responsible for freedom of action and expression. It is the hand on the tiller that steers us through the sea of life. And like a sailor tacking back and forth with the wind, we must keep our eye on the destination. We do that by constantly asking ourselves, "Where am I going with my life?"

We possess two kinds of will: *active* (outer will) and *receptive* (inner will). The active will, emanating from the center of the back (between the shoulder blades), initiates assertive and aggressive behavior. It can be used in cruel and manipulative ways, especially if one is unconscious of the motives of the lower self. The *receptive* will—the will of the heart—is in the center of the chest. It responds to intuitive and spiritual energies and is activated through prayer, meditation, and dreams. Both forms of will must be present otherwise we are unbalanced, a state that often expresses itself in physical disease.

THE SPIRITUAL SELF

Our spirituality lies in wholeness. As we unify body, feelings, thought, and will we grow in the spiritual dimension. The result of this unification is love: love for oneself, for another and for life in all its magnificent forms. From this spiritual place which we call our *higher self*, comes our creative power. This power gives meaning to our lives; it opens the gate to a path beyond material concerns, beyond the confines of personal reality. A path to unification with the great mystery, the universal spirit—God.

DEFENSES

Blocking Pleasure, Creating Pain

S exuality, eros, and love are the foundation of our reality; they flow through our entire being and bring supreme pleasure. Why then is human life filled with emotional pain? Why is pain a constant and pleasure so elusive, so fleeting? Pain arises from a deep split in our consciousness. This split causes us to fear pleasure. Let us take a closer look at the dynamics of this fear, our defense against pleasure.

THE DEFENSE MECHANISM
The defense mechanism is an inherent biochemi-

cal reaction. It enables animals and humans to respond to danger with either "fight or flight." To prepare for one or the other, the glandular systems of the body release hormones that raise the blood pressure, empowering and exciting the organism. When an animal faces danger, its hair stands on end and its entire body quivers. When the perceived danger is past, the hormones that aroused the system are broken down by other hormones and the body then returns to a relaxed state— homeostasis.

But if the organism is in a constant state of agitation, homeostasis cannot occur. When we cling to an imaginary belief that our life is somehow threatened we continually secrete certain hormones which create an imbalance in the functioning of the autonomic nervous system. This constant focus on self-defense creates chronic physical tension: the pain is a contraction somewhere in the body that blocks the flow of both psychic and physical energy. The defensive state becomes second nature so that when we find ourselves in a personality conflict, the images that perpetuate defensiveness arise again and again. We protect ourselves through aggression or by withdrawing to appease the imaginary enemy.

When we are hurt emotionally, our first reaction is fright, which then usually gives way to anger. The anger becomes aggression which in turn creates self-alienation because we are not living in truth. To be in truth we must accept the hurt; we must tell the other person how we feel. The voicing of our feelings not only creates a mutuality but also gives us the opportunity to learn about the other's intention.

The defense mechanism also affects the perception of our reality. When we defend ourselves, our mind freezes; we are in a state of shock and we focus on the potential danger. This fixation blocks thoughts and feelings, rendering us unable to express ourselves, unable to perceive the reality of the moment.

Spiritually, a defended person has no room for love and compassion—he is too busy defending himself. Eventually this state becomes a permanent attitiude. Those around him feel rejected; their attempts to reach out are received as an attack.

THE NATURE OF DEFENSES

Our defenses serve to subdue the forces of sexuality, eros, and love. But these are cosmic forces—they cannot be stopped or killed. They can however, be distorted and misdirected. When they are misdirected, they serve our negative intentions and become frozen into the defensive structure. This structure becomes a part of one's personality. Here is how a typical defense system might evolve:

> A mother who can't allow the unimpeded flow of her own sexuality, of eros and of love is faced with her infant son's natural expression of these forces. His outpouring of physical, emotional, and spiritual energy is an intolerable threat. Since she can't return his natural expression of pleasure, she must find a substitute—food or material needs.

Now the infant is a little boy and he has learned that pleasure must be stifled at all costs— it's *bad*. He adopts a strategy of submissiveness knowing he will at least have the pleasure of eating and physical care. This behavior produces the kind of person we know so well—the *good boy.* His primary goal in life is to gain approval. He becomes adept at reading the expectations of others and he imagines expectations where none exist. He bends every conscious effort toward meeting these expectations, imagined or not. His own emotional and spiritual needs become secondary.

The boy becomes a man but, of course, he has not extinguished the forces of sexuality, eros, and love so he must find pleasure in his negative feelings. He painstakingly creates negative images of others while maintaining a congenial demeanor. Underneath it all lies immense resentment which he can't express directly because he believes that would annihilate him. He expresses it covertly, perhaps finding ways to sabotage the efforts of others while appearing to be helpful. No blame can be laid on him—he's trying his best. But all his good intentions and valiant efforts to please (or not displease) never satisfy him or anyone else because his life is based on a lie.

The dynamic generator of pleasure located in his

core continues to emit powerful pulsations of sexuality, eros, and love—the greatest threat in his life. He exerts tremendous energy to thwart this inner current of pleasure and to fend off pleasurable energies coming at him from the outside world. He creates a fortress that is at once his castle and his prison.

Nearly all of the inner dynamics of his defensive structure operate unconsciously. He believes, he insists that he's a good boy. But the smiling face of compliance is a mask—an idealized self-image he has adopted to hide his negative intentions. His mask says, "I'd better do what Mommy wants. I'll pretend to do it willingly but I hate it—*I'll get even with her!*"

This ego mask is the outer crust of his defensive structure. He believes it and wants others to believe it; he is outraged when someone challenges it. This mask hides from him, and everyone else, a deeper negativity. He has unconsciously appropriated the genuine, positive qualities of the core, infused them with negative energy, and pasted them over both his divinity and deviltry.

His mask itself does not contain much energy. It

is reinforced by the energy of the negative emotions and of the core itself. Its only power is to distort and misdirect the energy that the core constantly generates. The mask is a house built on sand, its foundation a misperception of reality: "If I feel pleasure I will be annihilated; if I'm good I can fool everyone and get what I want. Neither women nor men want me to feel pleasure—they're cruel, arbitrary, intrusive, and controlling." Thus a fragment of his experience becomes his entire reality: not all women are intrusive and not all men are cruel, but he cannot make that distinction.

THE LOWER SELF

Beneath the mask lie our negative feelings and intentions—Freud called them the *negative unconscious*; Core Energetics calls them the *lower self.* Here all the rejected forces of sexuality, eros, and love are transformed into anger, hatred, vengeance—the negative emotions.

This self seeks the same solutions as the mask, but in a more primal way. Both the mask and the lower self manifest in the body as feelings, as thoughts, and as distorted spirituality. In reaction to a perceived threat or a rejection, an infant blocks the flow of energy, diverting it into channels that feel safe. This energy is made up of the same currents as pleasure itself, but it is thickened and deadened; the frequency of the vibratory pulsations has been altered.

Despite this negativity there remains a certain truth—the truth of our *negative intention*. The mask represents our attempt to protect ourselves from the recognition of this truth. But if we believe that it represents the totality of our being, we then discount the positive, creative, and spiritual aspects of our personality—our core. In this core reside generosity, courage, compassion, a belief in life. A therapy that does not include these in the work, but dwells instead on the negative unconscious, cannot lead to wholeness.

Though difficult, it is possible to face our negative feelings without being ruled by them. The recognition itself of our negativity, of the pleasure we derive from it, is a revelation. It weakens the mask and allows energy to flow. Thus the "truth" of our negative intentions is the truth that sets us free.

DEFENSES IN THE BODY

In the infant stage physical and emotional energies dominate; the mental and spiritual levels are not yet developed. The infant responds *physically* to any rejection of those energies. Therefore defensive reactions anchor themselves in the body and the emotions. The child expresses both satisfaction and dissatisfaction by crying, laughing, cooing—*physical* manifestations.

The child's initial reaction to rejection or hostility is terror. When the sweet, rapturous flow of emotion is interrupted, he immediately attempts to stem that flow because now it threatens his existence. Out of fear, he converts the flow of pleasure to negative emotions. These become the first line of defense against the outer world (the parents) and his inner world—the movement of pleasure within the child's body.

RESPONSIBILITY TO SELF

When we feel threatened by forces beyond our control, when we cannot accept an imperfect world, we form images that do not correspond to our reality.

For example: a woman is standing in line at the check-out in the supermarket. She suddenly feels a vague fear well up. She wonders about its cause until she suddenly realizes that the person in front of her, a tall, red-headed man, reminds her of her father.

But she also has other responses to men. She is married to a man who does not evoke fear; she, in fact, controls him. She must have everything her way, as it was when she was a child. Her willful insistence on *MY WAY!* reflects the frightened child within that must have what she wants, when she wants it. The demand becomes one for total freedom devoid of responsibility.

Disturbances of the personality stem from this evasion of responsibility, from trying to mold events to match illusions. It is frightening to let go of our illusions; it feels like we will fall into the abyss. But when we come to the whole truth about ourselves, we no longer live in fear. We understand that our illusion has led us to an imprisonment of self-rejection.

Responsibility to self simply means to acknowledge inner truth—our imperfections *and* our power, our beauty. To be responsible to oneself is to accept, without blame or guilt, the consequences of one's beliefs and acts.

BECOMING UNDEFENDED—
ALLOWING PLEASURE

When we recognize the ultimate reality of sexuality, eros, and love and accept our natural birthright of pleasure, we can then look deep within at the barriers we have erected against pleasure. The stream that moves negative emotions through us derives its energy from the same source that carries the forces of sexuality, eros, and love. But in its negative state, this stream is polluted, held back by a dam. Letting energy flow, we cleanse the stream of life—we allow pleasure and joy.

To a defended mind, filled with turbid emotions and distorted spirituality, becoming undefended feels like death itself. But it is not death; the freeing of our defenses leads to truth—our own truth and the truth of others. If, when we feel threatened, we can find the courage to admit our feelings, rational or not, we break up the stagnant energy and allow it to flow and cleanse

the negativity. No one can do this for us—neither therapist nor God: we must do it for ourselves. If we allow
the pain to tell us what it is, we learn its purpose. When
we loosen our resistance and observe the pain, it softens. The hard pain of defensiveness becomes a soft, healing pain—a recognition of the truth. To remove oneself from the arena in order to observe the pain is, however slight, an act of surrender. With this act the mask
falls away, the ego dissolves, and we can feel our whole
being vibrate with the free flow of the life force; now
we become one with our beloved. Now we can embrace
pleasure, joy—*life!*

SEXUALITY

The Creative Force

T he sexual force manifests itself at all levels of our existence: *physical, emotional, mental,* and *spiritual.* This force is the expression of both consciousness and energy as it reaches for fusion—unification. Although sexuality exists in all life forms, from protozoa to mammals, for us it has the power, through orgasm, to bring a transcendence of time, space, and duality. When it is unified with love and truth, it brings a fullfilment that soars beyond the limits of personal reality. To achieve full self-realization we must *connect* our sexuality physically, emotionally, mentally, and spiritually.

THE PHYSICAL LEVEL

Sexuality is born of a rhythmic impulse, a powerful yearning to know, to *feel* the reality of the other. The excitement of this internal rhythmic feeling descends into the genitals and leads to coitus. If there is no anxiety, no fear, then this leads to more energetic rhythmic movement and stronger breathing. Powerful sensations travel through the body from the center to the periphery and back to the center but at this point all movements are *voluntary*. The entire body feels alive, it feels warm, streams of energy flow through it; the muscles relax, the body becomes lighter. When the excitement reaches a certain pitch the movements become *involuntary*.

Now each wants to enter the other, to expand into the body of the other; there is a deep longing and an experience of expanded consciousness. As the involuntary movements become more rapid, feelings intensify until the whole body is flooded with sensations, warmth, excitement. Finally the rhythm reaches a peak and there is a tremendous discharge of energy into the other person. This exchange of energy creates a rapidly pulsating field of light which envelops both bodies. Then, after the peak of the experience—orgasm—the excitement gradually subsides, the body relaxes and there is a need for the partners to stay together in deep connection. With orgasm comes a fusion of all the levels: physical, emotional, mental, and spiritual. Although we hunger for this experience, we also fear it because it is a threat to the defenses we have learned to depend on for protection.

For this experience to be total there has to be a uniting of heart energy and the energy of the pelvis—a rare occurrence these days where there is much expression of sexuality and sexual technique without a true commitment of the heart. Our capacity for surrender is put to the test. Without love, however, surrender is impossible. Any attempt to surrender without love will plunge us into negativity. This negativity creates coolness, distance after sexual intimacy. Since most people are afraid to open up their feelings, their sexual experience is contracted, localized, and mechanical; there is anxiety and an anticipation of danger. The orgasm is confined to the genitals; the sensations do not travel all the way down to the feet and all the way up to the head. There is no heart connection so the partners separate immediately after release.

When blockages to pleasure have been dissolved, orgasm is much more than a pleasurable sensation. It is the embodiment of total unification—a supreme spiritual experience. When the forces of love, eros, and sexuality are united within us, we transcend personal reality; we become one with the universe, we merge in the same way one spiral galaxy merges with another. This experience is one of mutuality, not competition and it is a most important step in our personal evolution.

THE EMOTIONAL LEVEL

At this level there is the movement of fusion—the attempt to connect the heart with the pelvis. If there is real love between two people, it manifests as tenderness and as a deep comprehension of the reality of the other person—*who she is, what he is feeling.* This emotional level requires us to make ourselves empty in order to experience it in the here and now. It requires that the sexual act be natural, without pride. That a man not try to prove his manhood by "giving" an orgasm to a woman; that a woman not be passive and expect a man to "give" it to her. These feelings prevent a true emotional connection.

Because of various personality disturbances, many people do not allow their partners to be who they are; one tries to control the other. The full expression of sexuality requires that each person assert his or her rights and express them truthfully, without cruelty. We must take the risk of speaking out; we must make our needs known. If one partner is dominant and controls the sexual movements it will result in a withdrawal of feelings and lead to mechanical sex.

When there is negativity it surfaces in the sexual experience—attitudes buried in the unconscious are revealed. Emotional (as well as physical and mental) defenses are released which have a powerful effect on the other person. The guilt a woman has toward her father and a man has toward his mother reappear in the sexual act. If we do not accept responsibility for these feelings, or if we deny our own hatred, then sex will lead to hurt and humiliation. Many people have sex with their fantasies, not with the one lying beside them. A study has shown that in America, sixty to seventy percent of the partners are not present during sex; they go through the motions mechanically.

Those who cannot tolerate pleasure connect the sex act with cruelty and pain. A man unable to bring his anger out directly may express it in violent movements or he may fantasize hurting his partner. These are feelings he could not express as a little boy when he was angry at his mother. His brutality stimulates him (and often the woman as well); he feels stronger, more in control. But this expression prevents him from feeling genuine love for his partner. A woman who feared her father may anesthetize her pelvis, become passive and expect her partner to give her the missing feelings; she relinquishes responsiblility for her feelings.

THE MENTAL LEVEL

To achieve a mental fusion in sexual relations partners must be able to express their deepest ideas. If two people are not on the same mental level the sexual relationship becomes difficult, mechanical: frustration and anger ensue. Therefore it is necessary that partners be mentally as well as physically compatible, that they share their ideas, visions, aspirations, that they connect soul to soul.

THE SPIRITUAL LEVEL

Attainment of the spiritual self is the primary aim of life. This level of sexuality can only be achieved when the blocks in the physical, emotional and mental realms have been cleared. Once cleared, these three aspects unite and bring a spiritual fusion that allows the heart and pelvis to connect.

The ideal partnership has all three forces—love, eros and sexuality—fully present. Most relationships start with heart feelings but gradually turn into a state of friendship and sex without love in its fullest sense. This happens because the partners hide their true feelings from each other. He's afraid she will lose respect for him if she discovers he's been cheating or that he acts cowardly toward his boss. She's afraid he will leave so she does anything to keep him; she becomes passive. These barriers are like pebbles falling one at a time into a brook. No effect is seen until the day comes when a dam is formed and the water stops flowing. From these small pebbles—seemingly minor issues—a major wall of separation is built.

But when two people open up completely and reveal themselves to each other they create tremendous excitement and deep mutual respect. If he admits he's a coward, a cheat, and she talks about her passivity then the eros that brought them together is kept alive. The relationship is maintained through a mutual revelation of positive, creative feelings as well as shortcomings and negativities. Such an experience leads to a partnership wherein love, eros, and sexuality are united.

EROS

The Transformative Force

We have all felt eros in many ways. Its force creates a powerful channel between two people wherein a great amount of energy is exchanged. It shakes the body, it opens the heart—it transforms us. Eros is known to us in pictorial representation as Cupid, the cherub who shatters our defenses with the arrow he sends into our heart. This image shows us that eros comes from without—a gift that vibrates our core and produces an exquisite mental, physical and emotional bliss.

Eros strikes with such a powerful impact that it breaches the most rigid defenses. Suddenly, without warning, it shakes up your defenses; it brings movement, life and hope. The ultimate manifestation of eros is the connection with the force of creation. Eros transforms us from weak to powerful, hard to soft, rigid to flexible; it raises our consciousness to that higher level we feel when we connect with the creator through prayer, or the connection with nature we feel as we walk by the sea.

But some people, fearing they'll be weakened by eros, shut it out. Others plunge into it at every opportunity, jumping from partner to partner in their craving for the erotic experience. Their inability to develop a relationship denies them the experience of real love.

A BRIDGE

Eros is a unique experience but it is not love itself. It bridges the gap between sexuality and love; it spans the chasm between two people. The force of eros affects all levels of our being—it softens and frees the flow of emotion. Under its spell, a strongly defended man loosens his rigidity. He becomes a light-hearted lover; he writes poems for his beloved, brings her wild iris and seashells and whispers sweet nothings in her ear. Without eros he would regard this as childish nonsense.

Eros vibrates the entire body, causing energy to flow strongly, yet softly, in every fiber. The relaxation and flexibility it brings improves the sex life of semi-potent men and semi-frigid women. People under the spell of eros are radiant—their eyes shine, their skin glows, their bodies exude power and joy. They smile constantly and find themselves singing on the street. Warm tides of feeling flood their tissues, the stomach is alive and vibrant, the heart tender and warm. Their bodies seek contact and fusion. Eros is a powerful *physical* experience.

Eros dissolves suspicion, fear, and defensiveness. The man who last week told his male friends that all women are bitches now can't find enough wonderful things to say about his new "love." He thinks about her constantly and perceives a myriad of divine and delicious qualities. The bitch is now a goddess. A woman who believed men are cold and controlling now finds in her man qualities of tenderness, caring, and intimacy.

But these images—bitch/goddess, cold fish/warm-hearted lover—are illusions soon dispelled by the light of day. If our lovers believe that the bridge of eros is endless they will surely be disappointed. Having crosssed the bridge, the lovers must now work to awaken the more enduring force of love.

WHEN EROS DEPARTS

When we're smitten by eros, our defenses temporarily fall away. We're vulnerable; we allow ourselves to be seen. But we may turn and run, afraid to be so affected by another person. Fearing the same rejection we got from our parents, we retreat into pride. We act in accordance with what we believe our partner expects. Then we begin to anticipate his or her reactions so we can defend against the possibility of pain.

People with rigid defenses will attempt to maintain an image of independence by denying their feelings and needs. Underneath they're saying, "No one is going to get inside me." Eros can bypass this defense and enter at vulnerable points but it cannot dismantle the defense. *As vulnerability increases, the defenses against eros become stronger.* This makes the pain of a disappointing relationship all the more devastating. On the one hand it feels as though the other person is withholding the newly tasted bliss, while on the other hand the force of eros is trying to penetrate the defenses. The intensity of the pain arises from resistance to this force.

Eros is also a foundation upon which two people can build an edifice of love. But creating this abode requires a great deal of hard work. If the work is not done so that eros can be used to attain love, the relationship will suffer. One or both of the lovers will be disappointed and they will project that onto each other. Arguing and blaming, they can't see that the real cause of distress is their own inability to accept the expansion eros brings. Grayness and bitterness descend and, disappointed, they shut the door to eros. It then becomes increasingly difficult to allow erotic feelings to enter into subsequent relationships.

When eros departs, the effects may range from disappointment to severe depression. I have seen people open up, enjoy life and then later, in reaction, become emotionally paralyzed. Some have retained traumatic episodes from childhood—perhaps their mother's cruel threats or their father's brutality.

WHY EROS DEPARTS

Blocks to the erotic force are formed in early childhood. We create *emotional, mental,* and *physical* defensive mechanisms that are unconsciously triggered when forbidden feelings begin to flow during an erotic experience. When an erotic opening occurs, we open not only to love, joy and pleasure, but to the original pain— negative childhood experiences that have been etched into our soul. This fear, pain, and anger is very close to our erotic energy. We block the expansion of eros because unconsciously we can't accept the pain that follows the joy.

Defenses give us the illusion of security and control. Eros is intolerable because it is beyond control. In the outer layer of our defenses against eros we find images, "man," "woman," "relationship." Our personal images are reinforced by the mass cultural images we have inherited: men are dominant, women submissive; men are analytical, women emotional. Of course both men and women possess these qualities, but, the sexual revolution notwithstanding, these images still have a strong hold on us. They lock relationship into the familiar and thereby create an illusion of safety.

However, images are not the fundamental issue; they are the surface manifestation of the personality. The real issue is the fear of surrendering to our feelings and thus losing control. A woman may want something from her husband that she didn't get from her father. But her husband, raised by a powerful and demanding mother, takes his wife's longing as his mother's demands. They enter into a neurotic interplay which prevents a true surrender to their feelings. This example shows how reactions caused by images from the past adversely affect the present.

To find the real source of unhappiness we must transform these images and enter the inner aspects of our personality that hide the lower self. Then the real issues emerge: the woman says, "I hate men, I don't trust them." The husband says, "I won't give my feelings to her, she wants to control me."

KEEPING EROS ALIVE

Eros must be continually rekindled because it burns out just like a meteor entering the atmosphere. When it burns out, our problems begin: the one we found so alluring turns out to have annoying habits that we happily ignored under the spell of eros. But how can the flame of eros be rekindled? Through self-revelation. As we disclose ever deeper truths about ourselves—our fears, our inadequacies, our faults—we open our soul to our beloved in new and exciting ways. This is the excitement that keeps eros alive.

MAN AND WOMAN

The relationship of man and woman is potentially the most powerful expression of the forces of love, eros and sexuality. Unfortunately, this relationship also generates the fiercest opposition to these forces—two defensive systems interlock in a negative synergy. This "Battle of the Sexes" happens because of misconceptions we hold about the nature of men and women. Our differences are obvious; less apparent are the similarities. Not only do we have the same physical features (with the exception of primary and secondary sexual characteristics), but we also possess hormones of the opposite sex in our genetic make-up. Thus man *embodies* woman, woman *embodies* man.

THE CULTURAL IMPRINT

Laid over these similarities are the cultural imprints which dictate the social role of each sex. These mass images are created from the myths, attitudes and ignorance of the past: *men are strong, intellectual, calculating, scientific, creative; women are weak, emotional, intuitive, sensitive.* These images affect family structure and shape personality structures for generation upon generation. Over time, certain characteristics of gender become exaggerated while others are repressed or denied. Stereotypes are developed and reinforced by virtually everything in our daily experience: education, media and personal interaction. In recent times the Feminist movement has publicly challenged these widely accepted stereotypes.

But despite these challenges, many parents still expect their boys to be boys—*athletic, aggresive, in control of their feelings.* and their girls to be girls—*passive, emotional* and *sensitive.* A boy raised that way becomes a man who exaggerates his strength and hides his feelings; a girl becomes a woman who hides her intelligence for fear men will reject her. This denial of her nature blocks growth and breeds anger which she cannot express openly. Instead she directs it inward. She loses self-esteem, becomes a victim and blames men for her unhappiness. The boy, now in a man's body, believes he is entitled to anything he wants—he controls the world. Therefore he must not show weakness—it would destroy his self-image. Such are the origins of personality distortion.

SELF-UNIFICATION

The marriage ceremony symbolizes unification of masculine and feminine. But because we carry both physical and psychic qualities of the opposite sex, we have a need to unify male and female within ourselves. This is our deepest desire—to feel the vibrancy of eros and the power of love by unifying man and woman within our own body. To achieve this unification, we must remove the barriers that were created in our childhood—barriers we re-create as adults. These blocks, or defenses of the ego, create a particular fear.

The origin of this fear is the rejection a child experiences when he or she displays sexual affection for the parent of the opposite sex. The guilt created leads men to fear, and thus deny, their feminine qualities, and women to fear, and thus deny, their masculine qualities. A man fears union with a woman because he believes it will rob him of his strength; a woman fears union with a man because she believes it will enslave her. Hence the negative image we carry of the opposite sex leads to tragedy: a failure to consummate the union we so desire.

While man fights his feminine side, the main obstacle to his self-realization (and to intimacy with a woman) is the battle with his own masculinity—the fear that he will lose himself if he expresses his feminine side. He is confused about how much control to exert, how much to give up. If he surrenders, he's weak, so he controls and surrenders inappropriately. His lack of inner discipline results in chaos. This heightens his fear of surrender. Women want more control so they believe that to surrender is to lose control.

Control is the issue. As we increase our awareness of both our masculine and feminine sides, we begin to develop a more flexible approach to this problem. Once each partner can surrender to him or herself, a relationship can be created. To experience love and maintain a vital relationship, one must let go of the ego—*one must risk losing oneself.* By taking that risk, we learn to trust ourselves.

The unification of our inner masculine and feminine aspects is a spiritual journey that can only be stimulated and fulfilled by a relationship with someone of the opposite sex. And if a relationship brings disappointment, frustration and anger, it is still better than no stimulation at all. This is especially true for those who are just beginning to explore their inner selves because the energy of a relationship creates forward movement, an expansion of consciousness.

LOVE

The Unifying Force

L ove is the force that unifies the two fundamental qualities of life—*energy* and *consciousness*. Love moves the universe; it creates all that exists. Love is the supreme quality of God; it is a beautiful experience that we feel in our core. It is a force, a deep emotion which manifests itself through our intention. Without our will, our positive intent, it is impossible to feel love. We make the choice out of free will: *to love or not to love.* The choice to love is a creative act which expresses not only the will but also intelligence and emotion. Thus love is the highest form of intelligence that we can experience. This intelligence gives us the power to transcend our apparent limits. When we love, we see with fresh eyes, we feel with an open heart.

Love is not a given, it's a state that we work toward and experience gradually. It is difficult to achieve because when blocks in the body and in the personality are released through love, the freed energy will intensify existing blocks or create new ones to slow down the expansion—as we water the flowers, so do we water the weeds. Thus we are in continual duality wherein the positive (creative) aspect of life meets the negative (destructive) aspect. The task of our personal evolution is to move toward unification of this duality.

Love and eros are often confused. They are not, as most people believe, the same thing. When we say, "I fell in love," we usually mean we had an *erotic* experience. This is what ninety-nine percent of our popular songs are about—eros, not love. Eros strikes from without, loves comes from within; eros is of the moment, love endures.

SELF LOVE

Love brings you face to face with your *self.* It's impossible to love another if you cannot love yourself. Loving yourself means working with your body, clearing up your life, being creative, moving ahead. If you can't do that you experience neediness, not love. Your commitment and your will to love is the deepest aspect of your relationship to yourself and to others. Genuine self love is expressed by tenderness, by allowing feelings to flow into oneself and reacting to them. This way of treating oneself brings a balance between self love and the commitment to be in truth.

Exaggerated self-importance and narcissistic tendencies hide depression and unworthiness. True self love requires discipline, honesty and a commitment to confront the lower self without acting it out. Hurling insults is one form of acting out. Insulting, blaming and attacking are often defended as honest expressions of real feelings. They are judgements, not feelings. Unless the lower self is shared with deep respect for the other person's dignity, there can be no truth in the communicaton. And acting out is a form of self hatred.

It begins when parents disrespect and humiliate their children—forcing them to eat or get straight A's in school. When children treated that way become adults, they are unable to find their identity unless they confront their chronic negativity.

If we don't love ourselves, then we hate ourselves. Hate is a contraction of energy that creates isolation. When we hate, we're in duality, confusion, unable to distinguish right from wrong. We may get some excitement from hateful feelings but we pay for it in guilt and anxiety. If, in our early years, we have to survive by suppressing our true feelings to please our parents, then we create a mask behind which we say, "You don't understand me." Our fear of confronting our parents splits our feelings. Deep inside we develop an attitude that says, "I'll never submit." Love and acceptance are replaced by arrogance, self-importance, and power. These qualities are characteristic of our culture and they are expressed openly while others—hate, cruelty—are hidden by the mask. Even positive qualities can be used to camouflage the negative feelings because they are so difficult to accept. No matter what guise they appear in, these defenses are a distortion of love. The great human tragedy is the fear of experiencing love.

INNER CONFLICT

If we do not confront our lower self and our mask, then we project our negativity onto others and thereby create inner conflict—a betrayal of the self. If a woman blames men for exploiting her, she is not taking responsibility for accepting the role of submissiveness. By wearing the mask of blame, she betrays herself. Men, on the other hand, often act out this inner conflict by subjugating a woman mentally, emotionally or physically through violence. They refuse to accept responsibility for their destructive behavior.

These states are incompatible with self love and therefore block free expression of love for another. Inner conflict is a state of contraction; it opposes the expansion necessary for the growth of consciousness. This conflict blocks the rhythmic movement of energy, the very pulsation of life.

WILL, REASON, AND EMOTION

Love cannot exist without the active participation of our will, our reason, and our emotions. Love is generated by positive intent, our will to give, to understand, to care deeply, to express affection—to love.

Reason is the faculty that enables us to choose an appropriate partner: one who shares our values, who can meet our needs, who has a compatible lifestyle. Those who truly love are thoughtful, knowing; they have the power to transform their lives.

Love is an energy located in the heart center. When this center is open and active, it sends out a strong current of energy that integrates with other energy centers of the body such as the solar plexus (third chakra), or the throat (fifth chakra). It creates a powerful surge of energy that travels from head to foot and also outward in waves to the loved one.

THE STATE OF LOVE

When we allow love to flow through our life, we feel a powerful organic reaction in the body: deep breathing occurs, the heart expands, the pulse strengthens. In the state of love we strengthen the body, the emotions, we open up new vistas; we are infused with a divine energy, one that permeates all existence.

But we are afraid to open up fully and allow ecstasy, the supreme state of love. We constantly hold back and through our defenses we avoid a total surrender to our feelings. The work of Core Energetics helps us to recognize this tendency; it helps us confront the negative feelings we prefer because they seem to offer more security. This work requires us to open up our body, strengthen it, let it vibrate. It requires working with the mind, its images—distortions about our parents, our life, the world. And it requires that our will be applied to reinforce this movement so that we stay on course.

When love expands our energy, not all of it goes into the higher self: some of it moves into our defenses and intensifies existing blocks or creates new ones. In effect, this energy is turned into a denial of truth, distortion of feelings, repression that lodges hate, envy, fear, and contempt in the muscles. As this restricted energy ceases to flow, the possibility of a love relationship diminishes.

DUALITY AND MUTUALITY

The diversion of energy into negative emotions creates a state of duality: *I'm good, you're bad.* This duality can be unified through the power of our intelligence and our will. This is the task of spiritual evolution—the unification of the opposing forces within.

When we begin to understand how we contribute to conflict in our relationships and take responsibility for it, we begin to move from the duality of *I'm good, you're bad* toward the mutuality of *We both created this.* Then we cease to judge and blame. We move out of the victim role—we move toward love. For without mutuality, love cannot exist.

LOVE, TRUTH, AND FREEDOM

There is no love without truth; there is no truth without freedom. Our struggle is to reach for truth and freedom in order to remove the barriers to love. For some the challenge may be to open up their feelings, to cry, to have anger. For others the challenge may be to confront passivity or the need to control.

If one partner subjugates the other, there is no freedom, only dependency. This subjugation can be sexual, emotional, or mental. Everyone knows the kind of man who expects the world to serve him. He may be successful and respected by his community but to his wife, his children, his employees he is a dictator. He dominates women and expects men to submit also. If they don't he finds a way to "kill" them, by stifling the energy of love with rage and cruelty.

If one partner idealizes the other, doesn't allow him or her to have a full range of faults and shortcomings, it limits love. The idealizing partner looks to the other for energy, security or whatever need wants to be filled.

In order to love, the personality must be explored; we must look for the hidden, negative attitudes. It is impossible to establish love without revealing and transforming these attitudes of the lower self. You can pray in church every Sunday but if you don't examine what's underneath, it's like trying to sail without raising the anchor. Exposing the lower self is a challenge of the highest order: to make contact with the lower self without hating yourself; to recognize, to *feel* your cruelty without obliterating your personality. A commitment to the negativity of the lower self and the excitement it creates, blocks the feeling of love. If you don't want to love, you will focus on the negative, you will blame your dissatisfactions, sexual or otherwise, on your partner. If there is no love, there is negativity and with negativity there is guilt. Negative thoughts travel in a downward spiral and cause stagnation; positive thoughts spiral up and manifest creativity, joy, and freedom.

IN CLOSING

We embody a deep longing for the fulfillment of pleasure, a merging of the life-giving forces of love, eros, and sexuality. This is our birthright. But we find it difficult to love because we have created defenses against fear and pain in the very substance of our being. To love requires the exercise of will: to do our inner work, to acknowledge the whole truth. Without the inner work an attempt to express love produces a mechanical, masklike perversion of love. A fulfillment of love, eros, and sexuality is the end result of unraveling the defensive systems to which we cling. This work faces enormous obstacles. As we penetrate substance that has been frozen for many years, we encounter pain and terror. To further the evolutionary process we must accept— and honestly express—our hidden negativities.

We begin that process by acknowledging the beautiful qualities that reside in all human beings, by recognizing the wonderful soul movement of the psyche. There is no real life in us without the spark of love. As love fuses energy and consciousness, it ignites a brilliant flame that brings fulfillment and truth.

We are together in this life, each one a leaf on the great tree of humanity. The force that connects us all is love.

An Experience of
Core Energetics

A Workshop on Eros, Love & Sexuality

INTRODUCTION

Since 1983, I have led an annual workshop on Eros, Love and Sexuality. It is held at Trimurti, a beautiful retreat center in the gentle mountains of southern France, not far from the Mediterranean. The purpose of this workshop is to help people release feelings that have been buried inside them nearly all their lives. Not only to release but also to transform the negativity—cruelty, hate, envy—that lies deep in the lower self. Here people confront their defenses; they look at the mask they wear that hides their true feelings.

And as we explore the negative feelings that trap so much of our energy we also move toward a transformation that brings greater joy, expansion, and love— for oneself, for others and for the universal God.

I come to this workshop with no prior knowledge of the participants (except for the few I've worked with previously). I rely on my training and many years of experience to gather information about the people by observing their physical shape, the energetic and emotional expression of the body and the way they move. That tells me a great deal about their present state, their history, their childhood, and their conflicts. This information enables me to move directly into their defenses. The work is supported on an energetic basis through the body and on an emotional basis by directing the expression of withheld negative feelings into an open, creative movement.

The Trimurti experience is a gradual, methodical unraveling of both positive and negative emotions. At times we work as a group and at other times the focus is on an individual. But the person working in the middle of the room is not alone: everyone else moves, breathes, speaks, and responds in support of the individual's words, movements, and feelings. That way everyone can feel as if he or she is working individually. In a setting like this the work proceeds at a much faster rate than it would otherwise because the energy of the group is like a cyclotron—it is highly charged and brought into sharp focus; it discharges great amounts of negativity and brings out great quantities of love. The group accomplishes in six days what might take an individual months, maybe years.

Because the work is *always* anchored in the body and because of its depth and serious nature, people feel that they are in a safe space. The perception of *I AM!* is experienced on all levels of existence—we connect feelings, emotions, and thoughts *in the body.* This anchor gives people control of their being. They come to the workshop with a consciousness that allows them to participate in this experiment of life; they come with an intent—they are looking for something essential to their lives.

What follows are a few highlights from a workshop given at Trimurti. I ask the reader to bear in mind that a transcription* can only suggest the spontaneous expression that occurs in this setting. The work of Core Energetics functions beyond normal psychotherapeutic principles; it is an evolutionary process of the body, mind, and spirit—a creative act that opens us to ourselves, to others, to life, to God. It leads to a discovery of the higher self through an unlimited expansion of consciousness.

* The following account, "Trimurti: A Workshop on Eros, Love & Sexuality" was written by editor Peter Greenwood who attended as an observer and as a participant.

Peter Greenwood also worked closely with John C. Pierrakos, drawing the text for this book from lectures and direct collaboration.

TRIMURTI

A Workshop on Eros, Love & Sexuality
Led by John C. Pierrakos M.D., and Assistants

On a sunny morning in August, forty-nine men and women gather in a spacious, light-filled conference room. They're sitting on foam mattresses and large pillows spread out in a semi-ellipse. John Pierrakos, founder of Core Energetics, welcomes everyone to the six-day intensive workshop on Eros, Love & Sexuality presented every year for more than a decade at Trimurti, a retreat center in the hills of Provence. He smiles broadly, acknowledges a few familiar faces, gestures with open arms, and tells everyone how glad he is to see them and how happy it makes him to be so close to the Mediterranean, the sea he lived by for the first eighteen years of his life. He invites them, one at a time, to join him in the center to introduce themselves. As they speak, he holds each one's wrist in his left hand, closes his eyes and bows his head. He feels their energy and listens to the message carried in each voice.

My name is Heidrun. I'm a teacher in Munich, but I don't know if that's really what I want to do.

What do you want from this workshop? (Words spoken by John Pierrakos are italicized.)

I want to open more, to feel my heart.

I'm Carlos. I come from Spain. (He is a tall, curly-headed man in his mid-30's.) I started working as a body therapist about one year ago. I'm beginning to see how I run away from love, how I use my head, my thinking, to keep it at a distance.

(A small woman with short blonde hair walks toward John. She tries to hide her nervousness behind a precise delivery.) I'm Nadia. I'm a psychotherapist from Paris and I'm here to work on issues that relate to my body and I feel that...

John chuckles, *Oh, you're up in your head!*

(Nadia laughs.) Yes, and now I've started therapy on my body and I want to improve my ability to love.

Laughing with her, John says, *Maybe you need to lose your head.*

I'm Mia...from Stockholm...I'm a landscape architect.(She is short, overweight, and has a lively twinkle in her eyes.) Last year I found my body. (She's breathing faster, holding back tears.) I want to dance with it. I've tried and tried to lose weight but...

You have to do it from a place of strength, not as a compulsion.

I'm Rollo, from Geneva.(He's blonde, almost 40; his body is motionless as he speaks.) I teach fine arts at the Gymnasium. I'm very anxious about this workshop because it's the first one I do with my wife. What do I want? (He looks at his wife, a vivacious woman in her 30's.) I want a better sexual relationship with her.

Oh, you want to learn how to control her, eh?

(Rollo grins sheepishly.)

And for the rest of the morning, one after the other, men and women in their 20's and 30's searching for a career, a mate, themselves; men and women in their 40's, 50's, and 60's looking for a more fulfilling life, tell of lost relationships, lost sexuality. By the end of the week they will have confronted their attitudes about physical love and spiritual love, the lower self and the higher self, negative pleasure and positive pleasure, the intent, the will to love.

Now it's quiet. Everyone has spoken; the room feels different, softer. Tiny bits of the past and the anticipation of an adventure about to be taken bond this gathering of men and women who all seek the same thing— the fulfillment of pleasure, of love—of life itself.

The afternoon session begins with stretching exercises led by a Core Energetics therapist assisting Pierrakos. The exercises work their way into a jumping, stomping action accompanied by a rhythmic chant known to all—NO! NO! NO! At first it's a rote exercise but the intensity builds quickly and the uncommitted soon find their own NO! too strong to withhold. They are directed to pair off and express that energy toward each other. Again the chant arises, NO! NO! NO! It gathers more and more intensity and twenty minutes later, after a lot of steam and tears have been released, the exercise winds down; partners smile and hug, the group reforms its circle. John steps into the center and says:

This is an important exercise because inside everyone of us there is a no. An unconscious no. Even when you say yes, another part of you says NO! *And the unconscious no is much stronger than the conscious yes. We have to release our no otherwise we cannot say yes and be genuine. Parents, teachers, society have taken away our right to express all of our feelings.*

Now we'll do some breathing—another important exercise because we do not breathe freely, correctly. This incorrect breathing holds down all the stuff we got from our parents, from everyone. When your throat is blocked your feelings get stuck in the belly. We have to move those feelings out. Take four quick, staccato inhalations through the nose, like this—in, in, in, in (he demonstrates) *expand the chest and then release with a big, explosive* Aah!

(Again and again he urges them to take in and release.)

This exercise replicates, in a more intense manner, the rhythm of an infant's breathing as it alternately nurses and pauses for a few quick breaths. It fills up the chest with life energy.

With each repetition, the group's *Aah* gains intensity, volume.

Put your hand on your throat, feel the blocks and let your voice explode! Good, open your mouth, make faces. OK, now bend your knees and touch the floor with both hands. Keep your fingertips on the floor and straighten, then bend your knees again. Rise up slowly...slowly...put your hands on your waist, bend your knees, arch back and start vibrating gently.

(Groaning, all shake slowly and gently. John goes first to one, then another, correcting positions, working on the blocked areas of the body, giving words of encouragement, making contact.)

Good, now let's reform our circle...lie on your back, feet inside the circle. Breathe and relax...bend your knees...put both hands on your belly...explore it—start with the upper left quadrant. Use a circular motion and locate the sore spots. If it hurts, don't be tough and hold it in—let it out. A lot of crying is in the belly. Close your eyes...go inside...what is your belly saying to you? Reach gently under your ribs with your fingertips...let yourself cry...let it out.

Sounds fill the room as people feel free to express the pain of suffering withheld for many years. John continues guiding the group through a series of exercises for the pelvis, belly, chest, and throat—a methodical process designed to release blocked energy and integrate it with feelings. This process completes its arc thirty minutes later. Now the energy is contained, focused—peaceful.

After a short break, John asks for someone who wants to work individually. A tall, very thin man wearing a swim suit steps quickly to the center of the room. His name is Robert, his hair is short and uncombed, his gray beard scruffy. At the morning session we learned that he is a psychiatrist practicing in New York City.

(John faces Robert.)

First we have to look at your body to get a sense of what's going on here, You're a tall man and it looks to me like you weren't nourished by your mother so there's a lot of hollowness here (He taps Robert's sunken chest.)*...emptiness that makes you dependent, therefore very vulnerable. You look for this nourishment from a woman. Your whole body is contracted and you're blocked here.* (He taps Robert's midsection.) *You have strong legs but your toes show a lot of anxiety the way they grip the floor. There is an issue of security here. OK, let's begin with your body.*

John directs Robert to a padded roller, three feet wide, sixteen inches high—telling him to sit on the floor, then lean back with his shoulders and neck on the roller, knees bent and feet flat on the floor. The roller is used to elongate the body while breathing, opening up the diaphragmatic movement and loosening contraction caused by anxiety and fear.

Move yourself back and forth...keep your pelvis high...higher...that's it. Breathe in, in, in, in as the roller goes down your back...now make a sound as you breathe out—open your throat, let it out...release the stuff in your throat.

(John continues to encourage him and after three or four restrained attempts, Robert lets out long, open sounds with each stretching movement.)

Good, good...yes. Now show your teeth...open your eyes. Show who you are. Exaggerate the powerful man you are and that you show to others. ...Louder...that's better.

(Now Robert is roaring; John motions for more support from the group. They roar with Robert as he continues rolling back and forth.)

Work your legs…keep the voice going.

(Robert is roaring like an angry lion, pulling up anger from deep inside.)

Do you hear how much rage is in your voice? But your face doesn't show it!

I feel like I don't have enough strength to express it…

Yes, so you have to breathe like this—in, in, in.

(John repeats the breathing exercise used earlier and then turns to the group.)

That's why I started with the body—to charge him with energy; otherwise he would just be talking abstractions.

(He tells Robert to keep breathing audibly; everyone in the room is doing the same.)

React to your voice, your breath, don't collapse.

A memory comes of an operation I had when I was four. I was frightened when the doctor changed the bandage.

Yes, but what about your life now? It's good that you connect these things but what about your everyday life? What about your relationship? The important thing is who you are now! You're holding back your feelings. Can you say NO to your mother? To your wife?

NO! NO! Leave me alone...leave me in peace! (Agitated now, he screams.) NO...stay away!

Good...keep breathing. Let us hear your full voice!

This is the first workshop I've ever done with my wife so I'm holding back.

Oh, I see, well...say NO to her...say something!

I'm afraid to show my anger...I might hurt her.

And your mother too, eh?

Yes.

Give him the racquet.

(An assistant hands Robert a tennis racquet while another stacks mattresses in front of Robert.)

Your problems are not caused by your wife or your parents—they're in you. They are an emotional reaction, a

*response to situations in your life. So, take
responsiblity...open up to your rage. Can you show your
power, the man in you?*

(Robert starts beating the mattresses furiously. John
urges him to speak. Robert yells.)

Quit complaining!... stop whining!

(John asks the women sitting nearby to stand on the
other side of the mattresses, face Robert and talk back
to him, provoking him. They start whining and whim-
pering. Robert breaks into a sweat as he whacks the
mattresses with all the force of his pent-up rage.)

*Put your aggression into your lower body...push your jaw
out...move your pelvis.*

(Robert growls as he thrusts his pelvis aggressively at
the women but it's not convincing.)

I'm really ashamed to show that side of me.

OK, but everyone (John gestures to the group.) *gives their
permission, they support your process, right?* (They nod
and murmur a unanimous *yes*...Robert bares his teeth
and lets out a cruel laugh.)

Good, yes…there's the devil. That's wonderful. Keep doing it, that's why you came here—to explore the hidden parts in you. Now put your jaw out again, open your eyes…and move your body with that power.

(Robert finally thrusts his pelvis with some conviction.)

Good, but your true feelings are much stronger than that.

(Robert stops, he's pensive.)

What are you feeling?

I'm not sure…I feel very sad.

Yes, you have sadness because finally you feel alive…everything you've been missing in life—it hits you. When you open up your feelings, you feel sad because the life force shows you how you've trampled the flower of life. It is deeply sad, but it's very good too, to feel that sense about life, to become so conscious again. I think you have reached a place where you will want to integrate more— let it work in you and unfold as we go on. Is that enough for now?

(Exhausted but relieved, Robert nods yes, gives John an appreciative look and rejoins the group.)

The next morning, at five minutes before ten, most of the group is already in the meeting room. The rest are on their way, walking down the hill chattering in anxious anticipation or walking alone, silent, feeling the hot August sun of Provence on their arms and legs—a passive warm-up for the morning session. Fifteen minutes later, passive turns active as an assistant leads the group through a series of stretches and bends designed to move energy through points of blockage—calves, knees, pelvis, stomach, chest and throat.

John asks if anyone wants to work individually; a middle-aged woman with short, salt and pepper hair joins him at the center of the room. Her tank top and red running shorts reveal a well-cared-for body of smooth, olive skin. In her bare feet she is several inches shorter than John. They greet each other in a manner that suggests they've worked together before. John, picking up a theme from an earlier session, says:

Anna, what is this about not trusting men?...you roll your eyes at them...you're seductive aren't you?

No, that was an old game. I don't play that any more. (Her English flows rapidly in a heavy Italian accent.)

You don't? So what is it about this trust issue...if you don't trust them, then a part of you doesn't trust yourself. What don't you trust about yourself?

(Anna breathes a heavy sigh, thinks for a moment.) I don't...I'm not...I have no base.

So you're always struggling to create security one way or another.

Yes, but it's more than that. When I lost my friend, and then my brother-in-law...I mean...not that I'm thinking about suicide, but it's all so hopeless, so bloody hopeless.

This friend was your lover?

No, she was a woman, someone I worked with and my brother-in-law left a little boy so I've been with my sister, very close. And even that is very hard because on one side I receive a lot from life but I feel so guilty because I think I should be sending love and joy to them now that they're not here...I'm mad at them because they died. And my family never got so close...I mean the love I showed for my sister and brother and my family…I never managed to show it before. So that was a gift, in a way, but it was because of death. (Anna sighs deeply.) It's completely confusing and most of the time I feel guilty because I should send love and positive energy. (She pauses, begins to cry.) I'm not what I was and I'm not what I'd like to be…I'm stuck in the middle of God knows what. And I'm very angry…I'm mad. I don't go out with men anymore because I got scared stiff. So I'm mad at myself and everyone else. Foof! (She's growing more and more agitated.)

(John puts his hand on her shoulder and turns to the group.)

OK, this is what I hear you saying, 'All these things are happening to me and I can only react.'

(Anna objects.) But I can't control everything!

Right, but your feelings are not out there, they are inside you—they're precipitated by these events. So leave the catastrophes aside for the moment and ask yourself how you undermine your life.

By not taking responsibility for these things.

(John taps her heart lightly with the fingertips of his right hand.)

Or is it that you don't allow your love?

(The room is silent; Anna's voice is subdued.) Yes, that's right.

When you're in your head, you don't allow love to come to you...you can't surrender to it.

(She murmurs agreement; her agitation gives way to sadness. John directs her to a stack of mattresses in the center of the room, asks her to lie on her back and encourages her to allow her sadness to come. As she cries, he tells the others to allow their sadness too. Gradually her crying becomes a more intense sobbing; John asks her to use her voice. Anna's sobbing turns into shrieks of rage.)

Show your teeth!

(John gestures to an assistant who brings another mattress and holds it up at Anna's feet.)

Don't freeze...use your legs...move your energy—kick!

Move it out! You have a lot of rage. Keep your jaw forward. Can you give in to your feelings?

NO! NO! NO! (Eyes closed, she sinks back, gasping.)

Don't collapse! Now bend your knees.

(She resumes her furious kicking and they continue working in this manner until her kicking slows down. Then John tells her to take four, short inhalations followed by one total exhalation; the others join in, synchronizing their breathing with hers.)

(John gently directs Anna.)

Reach up toward the ceiling with your hands and say 'Help me, help me.'

(Anna is sobbing uncontrollably. She makes an attempt to say it but starts coughing. John turns to the group.)

When the energy moves up so strongly, she has that response in her throat.

(He turns back to Anna.)

Can you drop your arrogance, your pride?

(She starts crying again.)

Say whatever comes into your heart.

(She mumbles word-like sounds through her crying but she cannot speak.)

(Once again he takes Anna and the group through the staccato/release breathing technique. After several repetitions, John guides her back to a relaxed breathing rhythm. Waves of energy ripple through her entire body for several minutes. John looks at the group.)

Do you feel that energy? It's very sweet, it connects the upper and the lower body.

(The room is quiet, Anna's breathing is calm.)

OK, now stretch your arms up.

(He takes her through a short sequence of stretches.)

Now let it flow from your abdomen to your throat.

(He waits.)

Open your eyes.

(She opens her eyes and smiles. John waits again as the

experience settles in and then looks at the group.)

What's your reaction?

Her face is very soft, very feminine...
She's a beautiful woman...
There is a beautiful energy in her, but it kind of
scares me...

*If the beautiful part is allowed to flow, it's not scary. The
flow itself is not the frightening part, it's the anticipation
of something bad, something held over from childhood when
you opened up and were attacked or rejected. Now you're
afraid to open up because you think the same thing will
happen. But it won't. You have to dare to take the leap.*
(He jumps toward the group.) *Jump into the abyss!* We
think it's an abyss but really it's only this deep. (He holds
his hand, palm down, two feet above the floor. Moving
closer to the group, John continues.)

*These movements are natural body rhythms. They are re-
lated to the orgasmic movement, but they are not necessar-
ily sexual. Breathing, for example, is a pulsation—in and
out, in and out. Unless you're able to expand and move the
energy up, you're not performing the biological movement*

of expansion and contraction. An animal jumps like this (He mimes the action with his hand.)—*that's a biological movement. But we're stiff like this* (He tenses his neck and shoulders.) *or this.* (He shuffles like a robot.) *These blocks in our body destroy the biological essence of the movement.*

This is very important—it's what this work is all about—to establish biological movement in the organism and integrate it with your feelings, mind, will, and spirituality. If you cannot feel *your body, you're not spiritual in the deepest sense of your being. When you feel your body, your spiritual power increases.*

At the beginning of the afternoon session, John asks the couples to form two lines, men in one, women in the other, facing their partner. Six couples line up, almost shoulder to shoulder with three or four feet between the lines. Lissa and her husband Tor, both of them tall, handsome Norwegians, are at one end of the line. John positions himself in the center of the lines, looks first at the women, then at the men, and says:

Everyone bend your knees, bounce and breathe. Good, keep doing that. Now we're going to work with a certain kind of energy that's here, a withholding. (He looks at the women.) *You're holding back.* (He turns around, faces the men.) *And you too, you're holding back. You're all hiding a very important issue—"my way"—it's going to be MY WAY! You all say it, overtly or covertly. This demand is a result of your defenses. It leads to tension and arguments. These defenses have changed the color, the meaning of your life and your relationships. They are leftover strategies from your childhood. Your parents said, 'No, no, do this, don't do that. Don't put your hands there, it's bad!' That's our morality. But it's only a state of mind...it's not the truth. If you acknowledge and accept your reactive negative feelings, 'I hate you, I want to hurt you!' then you can identify the cause and free yourself. The recognition of your negativities provides an opportunity to work out your issues. We put no blame on these feelings. The goal is to express your negativity in this safe place, to open up a blocked energy flow, without wiping out your personality the way you did to please mommy and daddy or anyone else.*

Now, do you agree to be in truth? To say what you truly feel regardless of how much you fear it might affect your partner?

(They nod and murmur yes.)

But no name calling—'You son of a bitch!' and that sort of thing. Recognize your feelings, and express them, like, 'I hate you!' Use your feelings to maintain your truth instead of escaping into insults. Do you agree to these conditions?

(Everyone agrees.)

Don't forget that you do this work of personal exploration from your positive, creative side—it's your core that cares and loves and wants to remove the mask. The other attitudes of the mask are all distortions, no matter how much you identify with them. They bind the energy of our hidden negativities. So we have to open up and unmask those attitudes. Each one of you will now be both teacher and student.

(As he speaks, his assistants have each couple grasp the ends of a bath towel, twisted in preparation for a tug of war. John turns to the rest of the group.)

Now you get behind whoever you want to support and cheer him or her on, but don't make physical contact. You can switch your support at will to whoever you identify with at the moment. OK, couples look each other in the eye and say, MY WAY, MY WAY!

(Robert, the psychiatrist, is instantly yanked ten feet across the floor by his wife Rose as she blurts out MY WAY! A half-second later all of the couples are yelling MY WAY! pulling, slipping, sliding back and forth across the floor. The vociferous support from the rest of the group boosts the energy level; John moves from one to the other encouraging and urging.)

Speak!...use your voice!...express it!

(The couples struggle intensely for seven or eight minutes and when the energy peaks, John calls a halt. They reform their lines; everyone else gathers round them in a circle. Some are dripping sweat; all are breathing vigorously, eyes wide open. One woman in the couples line is crying.)

(John steps between the lines.)

This defensive position of controlling gives you two cents worth of excitement, right?

(He looks at the woman who is crying.)

Then it's followed by guilt and sadness because this is not what you truly yearn for...it's just a defense. You're defending yourself the way a child does.

(A man in the couples line.) I only felt my back, the power in it...I couldn't feel inside—in my heart.

Yes, because there are no heart feelings in this—it's all power, control, aggression.

(Tor) I just disconnected, I went ice cold...thought it was ridiculous.

Well, to the degree you disconnect, you remain passive and she takes over. You're not meeting her.

(Tor's wife Lissa smiles, nods in agreement. In an earlier, highly charged session they had confronted the same issue.)

(Tor looks at John.) I felt really superior when I was pulling Lissa around the room...

Tell her that.

(Tor looks at Lissa.) I have no confidence in you, you're so weak. (Several women laugh; Tor ignores them.)

I could throw you wherever I wanted—you're so weak.

But what about emotionally? Obviously you're stronger physically, but you have fear—where is your courage to stand for what you want?

I pretend to be nice...

Faking?

Yes, it's totally dishonest.

You're cheating her and yourself...your own beautiful qualities.

But I don't know how to do otherwise.

Stand for your truth!

But I don't know what my truth is now...the truth is somewhere there, with the women.

What's your truth? (Tor is silent.) *Do you pray? Do you meditate? What do you want? In your heart.* (John taps Tor's chest.) *What do you want in your heart?*

I pray to accept the totality of the forces of the universe.

That's beautiful, but what about your own creative needs, your will? (John puts his right hand on Tor's back, between the shoulder blades.) *Here's your will, directly behind the spiritual self. Tell us, what are your sexual secrets?*

My secret is to be nice, not violate...

That's not a secret! You're hiding something.

What?

Studies have shown that during intercourse about seventy percent of the people are not mentally or emotionally with their partner—they're somewhere else.

Oh, you want that kind of secret!

Yes, otherwise you're not being true. Can you stand for your own truth? Fight for it?

(Lissa objects.) You mean he should fight?

I mean he should stand for himself, not fight just to be oppositional. But he pulls back, he's scared. He needs to stand for his own truth.

(Lissa) Yes, to stand for himself—that's what I want.

He's afraid of me. But I don't understand—what's the difference between standing for ourselves and fighting?

You stand for your truth! You're very active here (He touches her head.)—*that's how you control him—but you're very passive here* (He points to her pelvis.) *and that expresses a distortion. If you defend that, you continue the battle. So it's not a matter of being* against *but rather* for...*for your own truth.*

(Lissa is quiet, the room is silent; John's words hang in the air. He turns to Andrea. She and her husband Sam, both Americans, have worked with John in previous years at Trimurti. She is slim, middle-aged, with a charged, anxious energy.)

Andrea, where are you now?

I don't have a lot of endurance but I have a part that says 'Yes, I want to win.' In our relationship I grow and he falls apart and lets me take over. So I liked this struggle because he stood his ground and I want him to...I really need for him to do it, he needs to do it. It was very energizing.

Close your eyes and look at how you create your demands and how he deals with them by withdrawing and controlling that way.

Yes, he's totally passive/aggressive. He's…

Talk about yourself—don't try to diagnose him. What are you?

I'm the active one, he drops away and I get angry.

So what do you want?

I want him to stand for what he believes so we can work it out together instead of me being left alone.

When you said 'I want to win' what did you mean?

There's a part of me that wants it my way—yes, it's there. When he says no I want to say it's going to be my way.

(John turns to Sam.) *And you?*

I felt good pulling. I enjoyed it…I liked…

Can you talk about your fear?

I run away, hide, withdraw. Then I get very sarcastic.

What's happening sexually?

For a long time she controlled it.

How?

I always had to wait for her, to tip-toe, to say 'Is it OK now?' I couldn't just put out my sexual energy. Or if I raise my voice she withdraws, pulls her feelings away from me and then I'm afraid.

(John looks at Andrea.) *Are you aware of that?*

I get scared. I know about it now but I wasn't aware of it for many years.

Yes, but his problem is he doesn't raise his voice enough! You use that as an escape. What about your own sexuality? Go inside yourself...close your eyes. Tell us about your feelings.

Sex is getting better...we seem to have switched roles over time.

Can you give into your feelings, let go—surrender?

Not all the time, but I do.

(John looks at Sam.) *Why are you so scared?*

I'm afraid to express my feelings

What feelings?

Of…ah…oh…

Let go, speak freely.

Freely?

On the surface you're a good boy. What's underneath?

Fear, inferiority.

Yes, only you can change that. What changes do you want her to make? You have to be clear and up front about it. Tell her.

(Sam puts his arms around Andrea, speaks softly.) I don't want to violate you in any way but I want you to allow me to bring my own energy to being. Let me be me.

(John turns back to Andrea.)

What do you want from him?

I want him to be the kind of partner that doesn't let me control him, that responds so I don't just go ahead and do it myself.

If one partner takes a position, the other cannot surrender—it's impossible. So you both have to give space but stand for your truth even if it hurts.

(Sam) It's not only with her, it's throughout my whole life.

Exactly. Your partner only precipitates that behavior. You two are together to be each other's teacher, to evolve. But we bring a lot of unexpressed anger and withheld feelings from our childhood. And we're always looking for the perfect one.

(John pauses, looks at them.)

You're doing good work.

(Sam and Andrea embrace.)

Yes, that's good, hold each other.

With each session the participants find themselves in a safer place, one that allows them to open to their deepest fears, their rage and their love. With this opening comes a new sense of responsibility, a new intention for change. In John Pierrakos' words,

> *There is an energy movement and a deep conscious-ness that develops in the group which transforms blocks in the body, the emotions, and the spirit. It brings each per-son in contact with the beauty and dignity of the real self.*

A BRIEF
AUTOBIOGRAPHY

I was born in Greece on February 8, 1921. My birth-
place, Neon Oitylon, is a small village on the Mediterranean with sandy beaches and steep mountains
planted with olive groves. It was tranquil and beautiful
but it was also a land of splits, a land of disunity. In the
middle of the split was the issue of sexuality. Men defended the "honor" of their women by killing each other.
We call it "machismo" and in Greece they call it
"philotimo." Growing up in that culture, I felt an omi-
nous force over me; the Greek Orthodox church con-
demned sexuality—you had to sacrifice the flesh to el-
evate the spirit.

I was surrounded by women: my mother, three older sisters, cousins, and aunts. They were caring and loving but they met some of their needs through me and with that I became dependent on them. My father was absent, traveling in Europe on business. He came home every few months for several days. He was the patriarch, very serious and disciplined. He never played with me, never told me he loved me. I was afraid of him, afraid he would find out about my burgeoning interest in sex with some of the girls around me. My mother was just the opposite; she held me and expressed her love. She called me "effendi," a Turkish word that means master. It was a common term of endearment for the first male child. She was uncultured but her love gave me security and, ultimately, the ability to freely express my love for a woman.

We moved to Athens when I was nine. It was a shock to go from village innocence to city life. There was no nature, no sea, no rocks to play on, no fields to roam. I felt imprisoned; I was so furious I would kick a tin can all the way to school. I played soccer with the same intensity—I would kick the ball from one goal all the way to the other. I had such fury and frustrated sexual energy that no one could stop me.

In 1939 Europe was preparing for war. My sister and her husband were living in New York City. She invited me to live with her—I was eighteen and she wanted to protect me. Soon after my arrival in New York, I enrolled in Columbia College. I took my entrance exams in French because I could barely speak English. When I heard that my cousins in Greece were fighting in the war, I volunteered to return but my request was never processed because by that time everything was in hopeless disarray.

At Columbia I had to study twice as much as everyone else to catch up on my English. And compared to my life in Greece, the freedom here was a shock. In 1944, while still in medical school, I was drafted into the Army and became an American citizen overnight! After I finished school I decided to stay in New York (instead of returning to Greece) and study for my Ph.D. in psychiatry—nothing else offered me such a broad view of life.

I remember the first time I got excited about this

work: I was fifteen, attending school in Athens, and I had read a magazine article about two men—Freud who had discovered the unconscious and Reich who had discovered "life energy." Reich's name meant nothing to me but my curiosity was piqued: *what is this life energy?* Years later, in New York City, a friend asked, "Have you heard of Wilhelm Reich?" I said, "No." She suggested I read *The Function of the Orgasm.* I read it and thought, "Wow, this is great stuff! This is an understanding of life at its source." After I discussed it with her, she suggested I work with him. I said, "Who, me? Who am I to work with this genius?"

I finally summoned up my courage and called him; he took me as a patient. And he gave me hell! He ridiculed the moustache and tailor-made suits I favored in those days. When I told him I wanted to see orgone energy, he took me down to his basement laboratory and put me in an orgone accumulator. I saw strange things—spiral movements, rays and foglike masses—I thought something was wrong with my eyes. I was disappointed. My scientific training in medical school hadn't prepared me for an experience like that!

I kept working with him even though I felt over-whelmed by his authority, his big face, his powerful voice—like my father's. I felt inferior; he provoked me to bring up my anger, my issues with male authority. In session he would have me wearing only shorts and ly-ing on the couch. He'd say, "You're not breathing!" Of course I wasn't breathing—I was scared stiff. Then he would ask me about my sex life as he observed my body. Occasionally he would put his hand on an area of block-age—my abdomen or chest—and say, "Breathe out fast!" Or he would have me move energy by kicking or by flailing my arms. He didn't deal with my personality issues at that stage of our work; he was only concerned with moving my energy.

In the late Forties, Reich was perceived as a threat by the American Psychiatric Association and others. They pressured the Food and Drug Administration to arrest him for transporting orgone accumulators across state lines. Although I was now a member of Reich's group and believed in the essence of his work, I saw that he and his followers were handling the matter poorly. I didn't want to jeopardize my medical license for an insupportable cause so I decided to withdraw. It upset me deeply to leave at that time because Reich had played a crucial role in my life; he had the fire within— that's where I connected with him. I was with him for two years before I realized he was the one I had read about in that Greek magazine when I was fifteen.

After several years as a staff psychiatrist at a New York hospital, I resigned and began a private practice in Greenwich Village where I was eventually joined by Alexander Lowen whom I had met in Reich's group. I was now married and had two daughters. For the next twelve years Lowen and I developed what came to be known as *Bioenergetics*. It was based on what we had learned about energy and character defenses in our work with Reich. It was very exciting to experiment with new techniques and concepts. We worked from the feet up and the head down, grounding the personality both energetically and mentally. But as time went on, I began to feel that something was missing in the work and in my life. My marriage was not going anywhere—it never blossomed into full flower, so my wife and I separated, and were later divorced.

Around 1964 a patient of mine gave me a transcript of a lecture given by Eva Broch, a spiritual channel who, since 1957, had been giving lectures (while in trance) on the spiritual aspects of personal growth: the connection of ego and universal consciousness; love, eros, and sexuality; unity and duality and related topics. She had created a community (The Pathwork of Self-Transformation) that studied and practiced these ideas. After reading her lecture I knew I had to meet her because she was transmitting elements that I felt were missing in my work.

At our first meeting her dark eyes sent soul beams right into mine; she was vibrantly beautiful, a magnificent being. We quickly discovered the complementary nature of our work and she started giving me guide sessions. These were not therapy—it was beyond that. Her guide would evaluate my creative efforts. Through her he talked about ways for me to integrate and personalize my struggle, my work. It was very exciting and, of course, we fell in love.

A few years later, Eva and I were married and around that time I left Bioenergetics to develop my work in a new direction. Those years with Eva were the happiest of my life. She was an artist and a dancer. One day I told her about the dance school I had gone to twenty years earlier to learn the tango. I was in a room, alone with a very attractive instructor and thinking about more than tango when suddenly a woman opened the door and said, "Is everything OK in here?" I said, "Yes, fine," while under my breath I was saying, "Get lost!" Eva said, "That woman at the door was me, I was the director of that school!"

Our work brought us closer together; she awakened my interest in the spiritual dimension of consciousness. I brought to Pathwork the dimension of energy—how it connects the body and the personality with the spiritual self. This integration led to a flowering of the work and we practiced it until Eva's death in 1979. Our love was precious, the way we cared for each other. There was a deep connection, total surrender. She was my soul mate, I was hers.

Out of all this—psychiatry, Reich, Bioenergetics, Eva's guide, Pathwork—came Core Energetics. The work with Eva caused me to shift the emphasis of my work from the defenses to the creative, the spiritual self. Now, because I have a deep respect and love for people, my interventions can cut through their defenses quickly and cleanly. I know in my heart what I'm doing and why. My ego is not in the work the way it was before. And I continue to work on my own issues about authority, freeing myself to be more daring.

I yearn to see Core Energetics blossom in many more ways in order to help unify the split between psychology, religion, science, and personal life. My work is to reach the depth of a person's entity. To help that person open up, transform—*move!*

For information on workshops, conferences, trainings, and research, please contact:

Institute of Core Energetics	or	Institute of Core Energetics West
115 East 23rd Street		P.O. Box 806
New York, NY 10010		Mendocino, CA 95460
Tel. (212) 505-6767		Tel. (707) 937-1825
Fax (212) 673-5939		Fax (707) 937-3052
USA		USA

John C. Pierrakos, M.D. is the director of the Institute of Core Energetics in New York City where he also maintains a private practice.